Easy-to-Use Sermon Outlines

Easy-to-Use Sermon Outlines

Russell E. Spray

BAKER BOOK HOUSE
Grand Rapids, Michigan

Copyright © 1978 by Baker Books
a division of Baker Book House Company
P.O. Box 6287, Grand Rapids, MI 49516-6287

ISBN: 0-8010-8143-2

Fourteenth printing, January 1997

Printed in the United States of America

For information about academic books, resources for
Christian leaders, and all new releases available from
Baker Book House, visit our web site:
http://www.bakerbooks.com/

To the men who took both my children from me,
And who hold in custody all four of my grandchildren,
Two of the finest Christian men I know,
My two sons-in-law,
Wayne L. Musatics
and
David E. Smith

Preface

Easy-to-Use Outlines are just that—easy to use. Simply add your own introduction and illustrations—and don't forget the prayer.

These outlines are designed for all who speak on spiritual themes—both ministers and laypersons.

My prayer is that all those who use and hear them may be especially blessed, and God will be glorified.

Russell E. Spray

Contents

1. "Amazing Grace" 10
2. Avoiding Satan's Snares 12
3. Be Your Own Boss 14
4. Christ, Our Spiritual Rock 16
5. Compassion 18
6. Coping with Care 20
7. Defeating Negativism 22
8. God's Plan for Your Life 24
9. How God Speaks 26
10. How to Beat Boredom 28
11. How to Win over Self 30
12. How to Work for God Effectively 32
13. Keeping Watch 34
14. Peace Through Christ 36
15. P-R-A-Y-E-R..................................38
16. Run to Win 40
17. Spiritual Success 42
18. The A-B-C's, Plus of Faith 44
19. The Dynamics of the Holy Spirit..................46
20. The Kind of Religion We Need Today 48
21. The More Excellent Way 50
22. The Need for Patience 52
23. The T-O-U-C-H of God 54
24. The T-R-I-A-L of Your Faith.....................56
25. Triumphing over Discouragement 58
26. You Can Have God's Best 60
27. You Can Win over Temptation 62

1

"Amazing Grace"

"Let us therefore come boldly unto the throne of grace, that we may obtain mercy, and find grace to help in time of need" (Heb. 4:16).

I. Redeems from Sin

"In whom we have redemption . . . according to the riches of his grace" (Eph. 1:7).

A. "Amazing grace! how sweet the sound!/ That saved a wretch like me!/ I once was lost, but now am found;/ Was blind, but now I see"—verse 1 of the hymn, "Amazing Grace."

B. Kings and presidents cannot pardon our transgressions. Silver and gold cannot buy forgiveness. Medicine and science cannot produce it. But Jesus Christ can redeem from sin.

C. Jesus Christ, through the grace of God, can reach down into the gutter of despair, lift up the penitent soul out of the miry clay, and redeem his soul from destruction (Eph. 2:8).

II. Relieves Our Fears

"What time I am afraid, I will trust in thee" (Ps. 56:3).

A. "Twas grace that taught my heart to fear,/ And grace my fears relieved./ How precious did that grace appear/ The hour I first believed!"—verse 2 of the hymn, "Amazing Grace."

B. Today's world is full of fear. Many are afraid to live, afraid to die, afraid of riches, afraid of poverty, afraid of youth, and afraid of old age.

C. God's amazing grace relieves fear. Since God is love, the more of Him we have, the less fear we possess (I John 4:18).

III. Reassures Through Danger

"For he shall give his angels charge over thee..." (Ps. 91:11).

   A. "Thro' many dangers, toils, and snares,/ I have already come./ 'Tis grace hath brought me safe thus far,/ And grace will lead me home"—verse 3 of the hymn, "Amazing Grace."
   B. Ours is a dangerous world. Without are storms, floods, thefts, murders. Within are trials, hurts, loneliness, and misunderstandings.
   C. God's amazing grace is sufficient for those who put their trust in Him. Friends and loved ones may forsake us, but Jesus never fails (Ps. 91:14–16).

IV. Rewards Eternally

"The grace that is to be brought unto you at the revelation of Jesus Christ" (I Peter 1:13).

   A. "When we've been there ten thousand years,/ Bright, shining as the sun,/ We've no less days to sing God's praise/ Than when we first begun"—verse 4 of the hymn, "Amazing Grace."
   B. Earth's treasures and possessions are temporal. They wear out, rust, and decay.
   C. God's amazing grace lasts forever. It is good to live by, and it will be good to die by. Christ is preparing a mansion for those who love Him (John 14:1–3).

2

Avoiding Satan's Snares

"Be sober, be vigilant; because your adversary the devil, as a roaring lion, walketh about, seeking whom he may devour" (I Peter 5:8).

I. Don't Stray

"Before I was afflicted I went astray: but now have I kept thy word" (Ps. 119:67).

A. Christians sometimes neglect their prayer life, and they fail to study God's Word as they should. When they do this, they begin to stray.

B. Some lack the courage to say no to non-Christian friends. They yield to the old life and become victims of Satan's snares.

C. We must guard our devotional life diligently, drawing near to God daily. We must take our stand boldly for God, staying away from Satan's territory (James 4:7, 8).

II. Don't Strut

"Pride goeth before destruction, and an haughty spirit before a fall" (Prov. 16:18).

A. Some Christians lack humility. They desire the praise and honor of people, rather than the approval of God (John 12:42, 43).

B. Jesus, our example, was humble. He declared that He could do nothing by Himself, but He depended on the Father. He pleased His Father. (John 8:28, 29).

C. We must be humble too. We avoid Satan's snares by doing those things that are pleasing to God and by giving Him first place in our lives (James 4:10).

III. Don't Stoop

"Be not overcome of evil, but overcome evil with good"
(Rom. 12:21).

A. The morals of our world are at an all-time low. Violence, illicit sex, alcohol and drug abuse, dishonesty and corruption in government bear this out.

B. Millions have relaxed their moral standards because they are spiritually slack. Christ will lift and restore those who repent and forsake their sins.

C. Christians must not condone evil, "but overcome evil with good." Assisting the less fortunate and sharing Christ with the lost will help us avoid Satan's snares.

IV. Don't Stop

"But he that endureth to the end shall be saved" *(Matt. 10:22).*

A. Some have made a good start but have come to a bad stop in the Christian life. Satan attracts, distracts, and attacks through his subtility.

B. No problem is too difficult, no trial is too severe, no burden is too heavy for the Christian, because God's help and grace are sufficient.

C. God is more than a match for Satan, and we are more than conquerors through Him (Rom. 8:37-39).

3

Be Your Own Boss

*"Be not carried about with divers and strange doctrines.
For it is a good thing that the heart be established with
grace..." (Heb. 13:9).*

I. Discipline Your Devotions
"I will... that men pray every where..." (I Tim. 2:8).
  A. Many fail in the Christian life. They do not discipline
themselves when it comes to their daily devotions.
  B. We must make time for God—to read, to pray, and to
meditate on God's Word each day, giving Him first place
in our lives (Matt. 6:33).

II. Discipline Your Doubts
*"If ye have faith, and doubt not... it shall be done" (Matt.
21:21).*
  A. Some people nurture negative thoughts and doubts. This
causes discouragement and failure.
  B. We must discipline our thinking, refusing to allow
doubts to linger too long. We drive away doubts by
replacing them with thoughts of faith (Phil. 4:13).

III. Discipline Your Desires
*"Set your affection on things above, not on things on the
earth" (Col. 3:2).*
  A. We live in a materialistic society. The souls of millions
have been captured by affluent living. They pursue selfish, sensual, and sinful goals.

B. We must discipline our desires (James 4:7, 8). We must guard against the love of money, excessive popularity, and illicit sex.

IV. Discipline Your Duties
"Do those things that are pleasing in his sight" *(I John 3:22).*

A. A lack of discipline causes many to waste time or spend it selfishly. They neglect church attendance and fail to accomplish God's work.

B. We must be faithful to God, allowing and making time for His work. We must witness to the lost and seek to bring them to a saving knowledge of Jesus Christ (Rom. 1:6).

4

Christ, Our Spiritual Rock

*". . . they drank of that spiritual Rock that followed them:
and that Rock was Christ" (I Cor. 10:4).*

I. The Rock of Redemption

*". . . exalted be the God of the rock of my salvation" (II
Sam. 22:47).*

A. Christ is the door by which we enter into salvation (Acts
4:12).

B. When we repent of our sins and believe unto salvation,
everything becomes new. We are changed (II Cor. 5:17).

C. When we make a total commitment to Christ, the Holy
Spirit cleanses us. This is part of the redemptive work of
Jesus Christ (Heb. 13:12).

II. The Rock of Restoration

*"And a man shall be . . . as the shadow of a great rock in a
weary land" (Isa. 32:2).*

A. Christ is the Christian's protection. When the storms of
life are raging He is our rock in whose shelter we can
safely hide.

B. Christ is the Christian's rest. When we become
exhausted by the hurry and scurry of our busy times, we
can find healing through prayer and the promises found
in His Word (Ps. 37:7).

C. Christ restores our strength in time of need. He is the
rock of restoration to those who trust Him completely
(Ps. 23:3).

III. The Rock of Resolution

"He ... set my feet upon a rock, and established my goings" (Ps. 40:2).

A. Many Christians are undependable. They are up and down, in and out. You never know where to find them.
B. Christ wants us to be established (I Peter 5:10).
C. When we give God first place in our lives and trust Him implicitly, He enables us to make the right choices.
D. When we are determined to live for Christ, He establishes our lives and keeps us from falling (Prov. 3:5, 6).

IV. The Rock of Rejoicing

"Let the inhabitants of the rock sing, let them shout from the top of the mountains" (Isa. 42:11).

A. Some Christians mar their testimony by wearing long, unhappy faces. They fail Christ, for He expects us to witness and work for Him joyfully here on earth.
B. Christians who are forgiven, cleansed, and on their way to heaven should be the happiest people on earth (Ps. 37:4).
C. If Christ is our rock of rejoicing here below, we shall also rejoice with Him in the life to come, for He is the "Rock of Ages."

17

5

Compassion

"But when he saw the multitudes, he was moved with compassion on them, because they fainted, and were scattered abroad, as sheep having no shepherd" (Matt. 9:36).

I. Compassion Is Undefiled

"And Jesus moved with compassion . . . touched him, and saith . . . be thou clean" (Mark 1:41).

A. Compassion means sorrow or pity excited by the distress or misfortunes of another; sympathy.

B. Jesus had true compassion. He was never selfish, never held resentments or ill-feelings towards others.

C. We must have pure motives also. We must care for others and give to them without expecting anything in return.

II. Compassion Is Understanding

" . . . he was moved with compassion on them, because they fainted . . ." (Matt. 9:36).

A. Understanding comes by seeing through the eyes of the sick, suffering with the lonely and bereaved, and walking in the shoes of the less fortunate.

B. Jesus understood. He experienced sorrow, loneliness, suffering, and death.

C. We should be understanding too. When we empathize with others, we are enabled to love with compassion as Jesus did (Matt. 14:14).

III. Compassion Is Undaunted

"... having compassion one of another, love as brethren, be pitiful, be courteous" (I Peter 3:8).

A. The good Samaritan became involved in helping the less fortunate. He didn't run away or look the other way (Luke 10:25–37).
B. Compassion calls for the courage to come forward to help with the job that needs to be done.
C. Compassion doesn't falter or give in to fear or failure.

IV. Compassion Is Undefeated

"... the Lord thy God will turn thy captivity, and have compassion upon thee .." (Deut. 30:3).

A. Compassion, like faith, brings victory. It comes from God and never fails because He never fails.
B. The Lord is full of compassion for "His mercy endureth forever."
C. Through prayer, concern, and effort we can be filled with compassion also.

6

Coping with Care

"Casting all your care upon him; for he careth for you"
(I Peter 5:7).

I. Some Are Care(less)

"... [the] city that dwelt carelessly ... how is she become a
desolation ..." (Zeph. 2:15).

A. There are many careless people in today's world. Their lives are in jeopardy—physically and spiritually.

B. Accidents are caused by carelessness. Financial loss is sustained and lives are lost through careless living.

C. Many are careless about spiritual things. They fail to accept Christ as Savior and Lord of their lives. Christians often neglect their prayer life, church attendance, and service to God.

D. God is displeased with careless living. He sent His Son to die for our sins. He expects us to be good stewards of our lives—diligent in love and service (1 Peter 4:18).

II. Some Are Care(ful)

"Be careful for nothing; but in every thing by prayer ..."
(Phil. 4:6).

A. Millions are weighed down with the burden of sin. This load is too heavy for them to bear.

B. Jesus came to take away our sins. We can be set free from the bondage and burden of sin by exercising repentance and faith.

C. Many Christians are filled with care and anxiety. They struggle through life, trying to carry their own burdens and the responsibility for others.

D. God is displeased when His people are full of care. We must cast our care on Him. He wants to relieve us of our burdens (I Peter 5:7).

III. Some Are Care(free)

"Stand fast . . . in the liberty wherewith Christ hath made us free . . ." (Gal. 5:1).

A. Many Christians are in bondage, but this is displeasing to God. It is His will that His children be set free.

B. Total commitment to God liberates us from bondage to self.

C. Helping the less fortunate, visiting the sick, comforting the bereaved, and sharing Christ with the unsaved brings freedom from self-centeredness.

D. Simple trusting faith—just taking Christ at His word—brings freedom. Only Christ can enable us to cope with care (John 8:32–36).

7

Defeating Negativism

"Whatsoever things are of good report... think on these things" (Phil. 4:8).

I. By Your Decision

"... Choose life, that both thou and thy seed may live" (Deut. 30:19).

A. Some people have a negative attitude. Their pessimism brings unhappiness to both themselves and others.
B. You can be optimistic. By deliberate action of your will you can decide to have a positive outlook.
C. Daily decisions are necessary to attain this. Concentrating on God's good plan for your life will bring victory over negativism (Gen. 50:20).

II. By Your Devotion

"Thy word have I hid in mine heart, that I might not sin against thee" (Ps. 119:11).

A. Many neglect their devotional life. Their lack of prayer and Bible reading brings defeat.
B. Devotion is necessary to positive living. Implicit trust brings peace, love, and joy.
C. Be faithful in your devotions. Keep praying (Luke 18:1) and believing and win over negativism.

III. By Your Diligence

"He that diligently seeketh good procureth favour" (Prov. 11:27).

A. Selfishness lends itself to negativism. Those who are concerned only with personal gain and self-interests tend to become negative when things don't go their way.

B. You can subdue a negative attitude by helping the less fortunate. Lending a helping hand, visiting the sick and lonely, loving the unlovable lifts your self-esteem.

C. Be diligent for God. Seek to share Christ with others. Sharing brings victory over negativism (Prov. 11:30).

IV. By His Direction

"I will instruct thee and teach thee in the way which thou shalt go" (Ps. 32:8).

A. Many depend on their own power instead of asking for and depending on God's strength.

B. God wants to help us, but we must do our share, for we are workers together with God (II Cor. 6:1).

C. Believe that God is directing. You win when you follow His leading (Prov. 3:6).

8

God's Plan for Your Life

"Thou wilt shew me the path of life: in thy presence is fulness of joy; at they right hand there are pleasures for evermore" (Ps. 16:11).

I. God's Path for You

"Thou wilt shew me the path of life" (Ps. 16:11).

A. God's design and order can be seen everywhere—in the planetary systems, the leaves of the trees, the flakes of snow.

B. The same God who brought design and order to nature also has a plan for the "crown" of His creation—you and me.

C. Nature has no power of choice. Man is a free agent. He may accept or reject God's plan for his life.

D. God's Word sheds light on our path. God's providential plan of redemption is revealed through His word. God's forgiveness, acceptance, and adoption are obtained through repentance and faith (Ps. 119:105).

II. God's Presence with You

"In thy presence is fulness of joy" (Ps. 16:11).

A. God has made provision in His plan of salvation for us to personally enjoy His presence with us. His Holy Spirit can abide with us always (John 14:16).

B. The Holy Spirit cleanses and fills us with God's love when we commit ourselves to God without reservation.

C. Spirit-filled Christians are joyful Christians. Their lives are purposeful and meaningful. They are guided and directed by the Holy Spirit.

D. Spirit-filled Christians are empowered to do God's work. They pray for others and witness to the unsaved about Jesus Christ (Acts 1:8).

III. God's Pleasures to You

"At thy right hand there are pleasures for evermore" (Ps. 16:11).

A. There are times in the life of every Christian when contrary winds blow and sorrow is deep and dark.

B. God's plan for His people includes "pleasures for evermore." There is coming a time when there will be no more sin, sorrow, and suffering.

C. Before Jesus left this earth, He promised to go and prepare a place for those who love Him. There He will live with them eternally (John 14:1-3).

D. Christians should strive to bring their friends and loved ones into God's fold that they may share His unending pleasures also.

9

How God Speaks

"For it is not ye that speak, but the Spirit of your Father which speaketh in you" (Matt. 10:20).

I. **God Speaks *to* His People**
   "I will instruct thee and teach thee in the way which thou shalt go" (Ps. 32:8).
   A. God speaks to us through His Word.
   B. God speaks to us through divinely-called ministers.
   C. God speaks to us through providential means.
   D. God speaks to us through His Holy Spirit.

II. **God Speaks *with* His People**
   "And truly our fellowship is with the Father, and with his Son Jesus Christ" (I John 1:3).
   A. God speaks as we exercise fellowship with Him.
   B. God speaks with us as a friend, for He is "a friend that sticketh closer than a brother."
   C. God speaks with us as a companion, for He has promised never to leave nor forsake us.

III. God Speaks *through* His People

"For it is not ye that speak, but the Spirit of your Father which speaketh in you" *(Matt. 10:20).*

A. Ministers and teachers should ask God's direction and then believe that God speaks through them when they preach and teach.

B. Christians should ask for God's guidance and then believe He speaks through them when they visit and witness for Christ.

C. Miracles begin to happen when we believe that God is saying the right thing at the right time and place through us.

10

How to Beat Boredom

"But they that wait upon the Lord shall renew their strength; they shall mount up with wings as eagles; they shall run, and not be weary; and they shall walk, and not faint" (Isa. 40:31).

I. A Change of Place

"I was glad when they said unto me, Let us go into the house of the Lord" (Ps. 122:1).

   A. When people are confined to the same place for lengthy periods of time, they may become bored.

   B. A change of scenery relieves monotony. A vacation, a short trip, even a visit to a new restaurant often helps.

   C. Going places for God offers the most effective change of place. Calling on others, witnessing, and winning the unsaved to Jesus Christ banish boredom.

II. A Change of Face

"A man's wisdom maketh his face to shine, and the boldness of his face shall be changed" (Eccles. 8:1).

   A. A new hair style, hat, dress, or suit often lifts drooping egos. By deliberately changing one's facial expression, one can actually change one's feelings.

   B. Stop frowning and start smiling. "Put on a happy face." A cheerful expression helps generate a positive attitude toward oneself and others.

   C. Hoping in God creates happiness (Ps. 146:5).

III. A Change of Pace

"The steps of a good man are ordered by the Lord" (Ps. 37:23).

   A. A change of pace is often the answer to boredom. Some need to slow down; others need to speed up.
   B. While temperaments and health conditions vary with individuals, feelings should not determine one's pace.
   C. Almost everyone needs a spiritual change of pace. We need to do more for God, giving Him first place in our lives.

IV. A Change of Grace

"And God is able to make all grace abound toward you" (II Cor. 9:8).

   A. Many Christians fail to depend on God as they should. People who rely solely on others are continually disappointed.
   B. God's grace is never a disappointment. Trusting in Him banishes boredom, for the Christian life is a continual challenge.
   C. God's grace changes darkness, drabness, and dejection to light, life, and love (II Cor. 12:9).

11

How to Win over Self

"If any man will come after me, let him deny himself, and take up his cross daily, and follow me" (Luke 9:23).

I. Definite Decision

   "If any man will come after me" (Luke 9:23).

   A. Many people have difficulty deciding which way to go. They try to hold on to God with one hand and Satan with the other.

   B. We follow the Lord through choice—"... as for me and my house, we will serve the Lord" (Josh. 24:15).

   C. We must be firm in our decision for Christ, leaving no bridge unburned which would facilitate turning back.

II. Daring Discipline

   "Let him deny himself" (Luke 9:23).

   A. Many people are self-indulgent. They fail to practice self-denial and restraint.

   B. We must set rules and limits for ourselves. We win by staying as far from Satan's territory as possible. "Blessed is the man that endureth temptation" (James 1:12).

III. **Daily Devotion**
   "And take up his cross daily" (Luke 9:23).
   A. Many people are devoted to selfish interests. They fail to win over self because they neglect God and others.
   B. We should be diligent in our devotion to God (Matt. 6:33). Faithful church attendance, daily prayer and Bible reading, plus sharing Christ with others—these bring victory over self.

IV. **Dauntless Determination**
   "And follow me" (Luke 9:23).
   A. Many fail in their quest for victory over self. They lack courage to reject the wrong and take their stand for the right.
   B. We must develop a bulldog tenacity, a never-give-up, do-or-die attitude. Determination, with God's help, brings victory in the greatest battle of all—the battle against self (Phil. 4:13).

12

How to Work for God Effectively

"Labour not for the meat which perisheth, but for that meat which endureth unto everlasting life . . ." (John 6:27).

I. Work with Enthusiasm
"For we are labourers together with God" (I Cor. 3:9).
A. Those who lack interest and fervor are ineffective in working for God. They give the impression that the gospel is unimportant.
B. We must work with divine inspiration. Zeal and enthusiasm bring results when presenting Christ to others. (Rom. 12:11).

II. Work with Earnestness
". . . The harvest truly is plenteous, but the labourers are few" (Matt. 9:37).
A. Many Christians are flippant and unconcerned. They fail to take their soul-winning responsibilities seriously.
B. We must recognize the importance of winning the lost to Christ. One soul is worth more than the world. Effective results come with earnest witnessing.

III. Work with Expectation
". . . This is the work of God, that ye believe on him whom he hath sent" (John 6:29).
A. Some Christians lack faith when working for God. They do not expect results, and they do not receive them.

B. We must work with confidence. It takes faith to receive Christ. It also takes faith to bring others to a saving knowledge of Him (Rom. 1:17).

IV. Work with Endurance

"... *we both labour and suffer reproach, because we trust in the living God...*" *(I Tim. 4:10).*

A. Many Christians take the easy way. They fail in God's work when endurance is required.

B. To be effective we must persevere. We must endure difficulties and distresses without being overcome (II Tim. 4:5)

V. Work with Enjoyment

"... *The labourer is worthy of his reward*" *(I Tim. 5:18).*

A. Those who work grudgingly are ineffective. They fail to display the joy of the Lord.

B. Working happily brings results. Many are seeking satisfaction and are attracted to happy Christians. God's children will be rewarded for joyful service.

13

Keeping Watch

"But watch thou in all things, endure afflictions, do the work of an evangelist, make full proof of thy ministry"
(II Tim. 4:5).

I. **Watch Your Will**
   "Then said I, Lo, I come . . . to do thy will, O God" (Heb. 10:7).
   A. Many people persist in exerting their own will. They fail to surrender wholeheartedly to God.
   B. Jesus prayed, "Not my will but thine be done." We can be a blessing only as we yield to the will of God (Matt. 26:42).

II. **Watch Your Ways**
   "When a man's ways please the Lord, he maketh even his enemies to be at peace with him" (Prov. 16:7).
   A. Many follow in the ways of sin and Satan. They will be condemned for wrong doing and sinful indulgences.
   B. God's ways produce love, joy, and peace. We become effective witnesses when we follow His ways (Prov. 5:21).

III. **Watch Your Words**
   "If any man offend not in word, the same is a perfect man . . ." (James 3:2).
   A. Some people are careless with talk. They discourage, depress, and destroy with critical, cynical, cutting words.

B. We must watch our words. Kind words glorify God and bring blessing, confidence, and healing to others (James 3:5–13).

IV. Watch Your Work
"For we are labourers together with God" (I Cor. 3:9).
A. Many Christians are busily involved in selfish pursuits. They fail to recognize the urgent need for soul-winning.
B. We must work while we have opportunity. We must put first things first, taking time to share Christ with those about us (Matt. 9:37).

V. Watch Your Walk
"As ye have therefore received Christ Jesus the Lord, so walk ye in him" (Col. 2:6).
A. Our daily walk influences someone each day—for good or for bad, life or death, heaven or hell (I John 2:6).
B. Christ is coming soon. He will receive to Himself those who walk as He walked (John 14:2, 3).

14

Peace Through Christ

"Therefore being justified by faith, we have peace with God through our Lord Jesus Christ" (Rom. 5:1).

I. Christ Made Peace
"And having made peace through the blood of his cross..." (Col. 1:20).
  A. Everyone wants peace—world leaders, church leaders, parents, children. People strive for peace through every conceivable means.
  B. Christ made peace by His death on the cross. All who accept Him by repentance and faith may receive His peace.

II. Christ Preached Peace
"And came and preached peace to you..." (Eph. 2:17).
  A. Christ's message was given to the Jew first, but also to the Gentile.
  B. The peace of God is available to all—black and white, young and old, rich and poor. No one need be left out (Eph. 2:19).
  C. Those who hear the Word, accept and believe it, may receive the peace of God.

III. Christ Gives Peace

"Peace I leave with you, my peace I give unto you" (John 14:27).

A. The peace the world gives isn't real or lasting. It fails to satisfy the longing of the soul.

B. The peace that Christ gives is what the world needs. It can solve world problems, church problems, family and home problems. It is a real and a lasting peace.

C. This peace is not earned; it cannot be purchased. This peace is given to those who love God.

IV. Christ Is Our Peace

"For he is our peace . . ." (Eph. 2:14).

A. To have true peace we must have Christ, for He *is* our peace.

B. If we are to have His peace, He must have us. We must give all to Him—our hopes, our plans, our will, our future.

15

P-R-A-Y-E-R

"Be careful for nothing; but in every thing by prayer and supplication with thanksgiving let your requests be made known unto God" (Phil. 4:6).

I. P-revailing
". . . as a prince hast thou power with God and with men, and hast prevailed" (Gen. 32:28).
A. To prevail means to become effective, to succeed, to triumph.
B. There are times when we must prevail in prayer as Jacob did. God does things when we pray persistently that He otherwise would not do.

II. R-equesting
"Ask, and it shall be given you" (Matt. 7:7).
A. Some Christians fail to pray as they should until trouble strikes.
B. We must pray often, asking largely. God desires our daily fellowship with Him in prayer, petition, and praise.

III. A-ccepting
". . . whatsoever ye shall ask in prayer, believing, ye shall receive" (Matt. 21:22).
A. Many Christians pray often, but they fail to receive from God because they lack faith.
B. We must ask with expectancy, accepting God's blessings by faith (Mark 11:24).

IV. Y-ielding

". . . not my will, but thine, be done" (Luke 22:42).

A. Jesus was facing the cross. His life was at stake, but He yielded to His Father's will.

B. Prayers will be answered; burdens will be lifted; broken homes will be mended; and souls will be won to Christ when we yield our will to God's will.

V. E-vangelizing

"The effectual fervent prayer of a righteous man availeth much" (James 5:16).

A. Our prayers can reach around the world to touch missionaries, loved ones, and the unsaved.

B. The prayer of faith is effective, both near and far, to sustain, save, and secure.

VI. R-ejoicing

"Ask, and ye shall receive, that your joy may be full" (John 16:24).

A. Rejoicing comes with the anticipation of answered prayer. It is an act of faith preceeding the answer (Ps. 91:15).

B. We must praise the Lord after our prayers are answered. God is worthy of our praise.

16

Run to Win

"Know ye not that they which run in a race run all, but one receiveth the prize? So run, that ye may obtain" (I Cor. 9:24).

I. The Outset

"Seek ye first the kingdom of God, and his righteousness" (Matt. 6:33).

A. Many lose the Christian race before they start it. They depend on a change of mind rather than a change of heart, or they base their profession on feelings instead of God's promises.

B. We win when we begin right. We must repent and confess our sins to God and surrender all to Him. Faith, based on God's Word, brings His forgiveness and cleansing (I John 1:9).

II. The Outlook

"Rejoice in the Lord alway: and again I say, Rejoice" (Phil. 4:4).

A. Pessimism brings defeat. Many Christians fail because of their negative outlook. They also discourage others.

B. We must be optimistic, looking for the good not the bad. We win when we reach for the highest and expect the best (Phil. 4:8).

III. The Outreach

"Now then we are ambassadors for Christ..." (II Cor. 5:20).

A. Many fail because of self-centeredness. They seek only temporal and selfish gains.

B. We win in the Christian life by reaching out to others, helping the less fortunate, and witnessing to the lost (Phil. 2:16).

IV. The Outcome

"I have finished my course.... Henceforth there is laid up for me a crown of righteousness..." (II Tim. 4:7, 8).

A. Those who reject Christ will lose the race. Their destiny will be sealed.

B. Those who accept Christ will be rewarded with the crown of life and eternity with God.

C. The outset, outlook, and outreach determine the outcome (John 14:2, 3).

17

Spiritual Success

"For then thou shalt make thy way prosperous, and then thou shalt have good success" (Josh. 1:8).

I. **Commitment to Christ**

   "... I pray God your whole spirit and soul and body be preserved blameless ..." (I Thess. 5:23).

   A. Some Christians fall short of pleasing God because they are not totally committed to Him. They insist on asserting their will over God's will.

   B. Spiritual success demands complete abandonment of self and the acceptance of God's will. His will makes everything work together for our good and His glory (Rom. 8:28).

II. **Confidence in Christ**

   "... this is the confidence that we have in him, that, if we ask anything according to his will, he heareth us" (I John 5:14).

   A. World and national conditions have caused a breakdown in trust and confidence. This holds true in government, business, school, church, and family.

   B. Christ is still the Truth. We can safely place our confidence in Him. He never misrepresents or undermines. Trusting Christ leads to spiritual success.

III. **Compassion Like Christ's**

   "... when the Lord saw her, he had compassion on her, and said unto her, Weep not" (Luke 7:13).

   A. Jesus had great compassion. Because He was touched by

the infirmities of others, He healed the lame, the halt, and the blind.

B. We attain spiritual success when we are compassionate— pray for the sick, help the needy, and comfort the bereaved.

IV. Cooperation with Christ

"We then [are] as workers together with him . . ." (II Cor. 6:1).

A. Many Christians fail to work for Christ as they should. They neglect, make excuses, and fail to cooperate with Christ in carrying out His commission.

B. When we work *for* Christ, we are working *with* Him also. He goes with us and speaks through us as we call, invite, and witness.

V. Contentment Through Christ

"For I have learned, in whatsoever state I am, therewith to be content" (Phil. 4:11).

A. Discontentment is prevalent in today's world. Many are trying to find contentment through possessions, pleasures, and popularity.

B. Real and lasting contentment is found only in Jesus Christ. He satisfies the longing of the soul and brings spiritual success (I Tim. 6:6).

18

The A-B-C's, Plus of Faith

"Now faith is the substance of things hoped for, the evidence of things not seen" (Heb. 11:1).

I. A-sking of Faith
"But let him ask in faith, nothing wavering" (James 1:6).
A. Many fail to receive from God simply because they do not ask (Matt. 7:7).
B. We are to ask in childlike faith. Just as earthly parents want to give good gifts to their children, so our Heavenly Father desires to do the same for His children (Matt. 7:11).
C. Children are persistent. With a child's persistence we must keep on asking our heavenly Father (Matt. 7:8).

II. B-elieving of Faith
". . . Believe that ye receive them, and ye shall have them" (Mark 11:24).
A. Some have difficulty believing. Their doubts cause them to live a defeated life.
B. Everyone is tempted to doubt at times, but we must keep on believing in spite of doubts. We defeat Satan by believing that we believe.
C. Everything is possible for those who believe (Matt. 9:28, 29). Faith pleases God and brings His blessings (Heb. 11:6).

III. C-onfessing of Faith

"... with the mouth confession is made unto salvation"
(Rom. 10:10).

A. Some people are ashamed to be called Christians. They are fearful of scorn and persecution.

B. We must be courageous about confessing our faith in Jesus Christ. If we are ashamed of Him, He will be ashamed of us also (Mark 8:38).

C. Salvation depends upon the confession of our faith. We must be willing to share Christ with others (Rom. 1:16).

IV. D-oing of Faith

"... faith without works is dead" *(James 2:20).*

A. Doing is the "plus" of faith. Many falter in the Christian life because they fail to *act upon* or *work their faith.*

B. We must let the Holy Spirit work through us. We are His channel, the instrument through which He works.

C. We must believe that the Holy Spirit is directing and guiding our steps. He speaks through us as we witness to the unsaved (John 15:5).

19

The Dynamics of the Holy Spirit

"And suddenly there came a sound from heaven as of a rushing, mighty wind. . . . And they were all filled with the Holy Ghost . . ." (Acts 2:2–4).

I. **The Holy Spirit Convicts**

"And when He is come, he will reprove the world of sin . . ." (John 16:8).

A. The Holy Spirit convicts of sin and wrong doing. Many fail to respond to His reproof but continue to practice their sinful ways. Unless they repent, they are doomed to eternal death.

B. When the Holy Spirit reproves us for wrong words, thoughts, deeds, and actions, we must ask for His forgiveness and cleansing.

II. **The Holy Spirit Converts**

"Repent, and be baptized . . . in the name of Jesus Christ for the remission of sins . . ." (Acts 2:38).

A. Repentance and faith bring forgiveness of sins. The Holy Spirit bears witness through the spirit of one who has become a member of the family of God.

B. Conversion brings new life in Christ. It gives a new faith, new hope, and new love, for "old things are passed away" (II Cor. 5:17).

III. **The Holy Spirit Cleanses**

". . . purifying their hearts by faith" (Acts 15:9).

A. Some Christians fail to make a total commitment to Christ. They are unwilling to give up certain things for Christ—habits, affections, or possessions.

B. We must surrender everything unreservedly to Christ. When we are willing to yield all to Him, the Holy Spirit is ready to cleanse and fill us with His love (I John 1:7).

IV. **The Holy Spirit Comforts**

"... *he shall give you another Comforter, that he may abide with you for ever" (John 14:16)*.

A. There is little comfort in today's world. War threats, separations, divorces, shortages, and inflation bring frustration and disappointment.

B. Christians are confronted with difficulties also, but they can possess the peace and comfort that only the presence of the Holy Spirit can bring.

V. **The Holy Spirit Controls**

"Howbeit when he, the Spirit of truth, is come, he will guide you into all truth" (John 16:13).

A. Many try to live their lives depending on their own strength. They fail because finite power is not sufficient for successful living.

B. We need the guidance and direction of the Holy Spirit. God is omniscient and omnipotent. He gives those who are totally committed the power needed for service. He assures them of eternal life hereafter (Acts 1:8).

20

The Kind of Religion
We Need Today

"Pure religion and undefiled before God and the Father is this . . . to keep himself unspotted from the world" (James 1:27).

I. Personal Religion

"Except a man be born again, he cannot see the kingdom of God" (John 3:3).

A. Many in today's world profess religion but have never experienced a spiritual and personal encounter with Jesus Christ.

B. We must be "born again" through repentance and faith. When God forgives our sins, He receives us into the family of God (Luke 13:3-5).

II. Purifying Religion

". . . the blood of Jesus Christ his Son cleanseth us from all sin" (I John 1:7).

A. Many Christians have never totally committed their lives to Jesus Christ. They falter because they persist in having their own way.

B. We must surrender our will unreservedly to God's will. Doing so brings cleansing and the presence of the Holy Spirit (I Thess. 5:23).

III. Positive Religion

"We know that we have passed from death unto life . . ." (I John 3:14).

A. There is a lack of sureness in today's religion. Many are vague and uncertain about their spiritual state. They declare, "I *guess* so," or "I *hope* so."

B. We can be positive, for we "know [in whom we] have believed." No argument can refute the "I know," or "I have " response (II Tim. 1:12).

IV. Powerful Religion

"Who are kept by the power of God through faith..." *(I Peter 1:5).*

A. Much modern religion makes no claims concerning its power to save, sanctify, and sustain. It is a powerless religion.

B. The need is for a religion with power—God's power. He is able to forgive sins, cleanse hearts, heal the sick, and "keep that which [we] have committed unto him..." (II Tim. 1:12).

V. Productive Religion

"... I have chosen you ... that ye should go and bring forth fruit..." *(John 15:16).*

A. Many Christians fail to work diligently for God. Some are unconcerned; some are neglectful. Others are spiritually lazy.

B. We must be about the Master's business. Jesus is coming soon. We should pray for the needs of others, assist the less fortunate, and share Christ with the unsaved (Acts 1:8).

21

The More Excellent Way

I Corinthians 13

"And yet shew I unto you a more excellent way" (I Cor. 12:31).

I. The Value of Love (I Cor. 13:1–3)

"...and have not charity [love], it profiteth me nothing" (I Cor. 13:3).

A. The value of love is beyond estimation. No gift or possession is profitable without it.

B. In these verses Paul compares the superiority of love to the gift of languages, the gift of prophecy, miraculous faith, and the doing of sacrifices and good deeds.

C. We must recognize the value of love also, for God's love enables us to do His work effectively. God is love and the more like Him we become, the more love we will possess.

II. The Virtues of Love (I Cor. 13:4–7)

"... beareth... believeth... hopeth... endureth all things" (I Cor. 13:7).

A. The virtues of love include kindness, humility, selflessness, patience, compassion, faith, and love.

B. Many people are trying to express the virtues of love without the possession of love. This is impossible to do.

C. We must possess the Spirit of Christ if we are to succeed in performing the work of Christ. Being filled with the Holy Spirit enables us to practice the virtues of love.

III. The Victory of Love (I Cor. 13:8-13)
"But the greatest of these is [love]" (I Cor. 13:13).

A. Loved ones, friends, pleasures, and possessions sometimes fail, but "love never faileth."

B. Faith pleases God, but faith serves its purpose only in this life. We cannot live without hope, but hope will not be needed in the world to come.

C. Love is a necessity; everyone needs to love and be loved. Love is eternal; it will unfold in greater beauty and glory while endless ages roll. Victory is assured those who are filled with God's love.

22

The Need for Patience

"For ye have need of patience, that, after ye have done the will of God, ye might receive the promise" (Heb. 10:36).

I. Patience in Suffering

"Ye have heard of the patience of Job . . ." (James 5:11).

A. Job was patient in suffering. He won the approval and blessing of God through his trust and determination (Job 13:15).

B. We should also be patient in suffering. We should look for its purpose and seek to glorify God through it.

II. Patience in Sorrow

"I waited patiently for the Lord; and he . . . heard my cry" (Ps. 40:1).

A. Jesus was a man of sorrow. He bore deception, disgrace, and death with patience, compassion, and forgiveness.

B. We should also be patient in sorrow. We should endure trials, troubles, and testings as Jesus did (Eph. 4:32).

III. Patience in Success

". . . let us run with patience the race that is set before us" (Heb. 12:1).

A. Patience is needed in attaining success. Overconfidence and overwork are to be avoided.

B. Patience is needed when success has been attained. A person's motives may be misjudged by others, but God looks on the heart (I Sam. 16:7).

IV. Patience in Setbacks
"Rest in the Lord, and wait patiently for him" (Ps. 37:7).
- A. Setbacks are difficult to bear. They bring feelings of discouragement, defeat, and humiliation.
- B. God has a purpose in allowing setbacks. We must trust in Him, knowing that His ways are always best. We must wait patiently for His will to be revealed (Rom. 8:28).

V. Patience in Service
"And so, after he had patiently endured, he obtained the promise" (Heb. 6:15).
- A. Service should be performed as unto the Lord. The more we do, the more criticism we often receive from other people.
- B. Perseverance is needed when results are slow in coming. Patience is needed in all our service for God (Col. 3:23, 24).

23

The T-O-U-C-H of God

"And there went with him a band of men, whose hearts God had touched" (I Sam. 10:26).

I. T-ransforms

". . . if any man be in Christ, he is a new creature" (II Cor. 5:17).

- A. The touch of God brings forgiveness of sins to those who repent and believe. It brings cleansing and power to those who yield themselves totally to God.
- B. The transforming touch of God makes everything new. We receive a new life in Christ Jesus, new desires, new activities, and a new hope of eternal life (II Cor. 5:17).

II. O-rdains

". . . I have . . . ordained you, that ye should go and bring forth fruit . . ." (John 15:16).

- A. Many Christians fail because they do not work for God. Some think only ministers are to witness to the unsaved and win them to Christ.
- B. The touch of God ordains all Christians into God's service. Everyone can share something for God—a smile, a prayer, a helping hand.

III. U-nifies

". . . how good . . . it is for brethren to dwell together in unity!" (Ps. 133:1).

- A. Many churches fail because their members do not work together; they are divided. Some pull in one direction, and others in another direction.

B. The touch of God brings harmony and love. It enables us to accomplish God's work in "the unity of the Spirit" (Eph. 4:2, 3).

IV. C-onquers

"... we are more than conquerors through him that loved us" (Rom. 8:37).

A. Many Christians give up too easily. They throw up their hands and quit when they are persecuted, rebuked, or when they fail to get their own way.

B. The touch of God gives us courage to conquer. Christ furnishes the strength which enables us to "keep on keeping on" (Phil. 4:13).

V. H-eals

"And Jesus put forth his hand, and touched him ..." (Matt. 8:3).

A. Many have never experienced divine healing because of a lack of faith. We cannot expect to please God or receive blessings from Him without faith (Heb. 11:6).

B. The touch of God brings physical, mental, and spiritual healing. We receive God's touch through reading His Word, praying, believing, accepting, and obeying (Matt. 9:29).

24

The T-R-I-A-L of Your Faith

"That the trial of your faith, being much more precious than of gold that perisheth, though it be tried with fire, might be found unto praise and honour and glory at the appearing of Jesus Christ" (I Peter 1:7).

I. T-emptation
"The Lord knoweth how to deliver the godly out of temptations . . ." (II Peter 2:9).
 A. Every Christian experiences temptation. Satan tries to catch Christians unawares.
 B. We must not yield to temptation. We can overcome through decision, discipline, determination, and divine help (James 1:12).

II. R-esentment
"He that loveth not his brother abideth in death" (I John 3:14).
 A. Resentments dwindle the physical, dwarf the mental, and destroy the spiritual life of an individual.
 B. We can be released from resentments through love and prayer. One cannot love and pray for another person and hold resentments at the same time.

III. I-nferiority
"I can do all things through Christ which strengtheneth me" (Phil. 4:13).
 A. Inferiority feelings hinder Christians from working for God as they should.

B. We overcome by doing, by moving ahead, by believing the Holy Spirit is within us, and that He is guiding, directing, and speaking through us.

IV. A-ffliction
"Before I was afflicted I went astray: but now have I kept thy word" (Ps. 119:67).
A. Christians suffer affliction like everyone else. Some blame God when they suffer.
B. We must trust God during affliction. He has a purpose in what He allows and can work it out for our good and His glory (Rom. 8:28).

V. L-oneliness
". . . I will never leave thee, nor forsake thee" (Heb. 13:5).
A. Many people are lonely. Sin, sorrow, suffering, and separation bring loneliness.
B. Christians need never be lonely. They have a "friend who is closer than a brother." The Holy Spirit promised to "abide with them forever" (John 14:16).

25

Triumphing over Discouragement

"Why art thou cast down, O my soul? and why art thou disquieted in me? hope thou in God: for I shall yet praise him . . ." (Ps. 42:5).

I. Don't Give In to It

"Resist the devil, and he will flee from you" (James 4:7).

A. Many people give in to discouragement because they lack discipline and self-control.

B. We must exert our will power when it comes to discouragement. Determination and faith bring God's power and help us win (James 1:12).

II. Don't Give Out with It

"Talk ye of all his wondrous work" (Ps. 105:2).

A. Some people are negative. Their pessimistic thoughts and words bring discouragement to themselves and to others.

B. We must be positive—look for the good, not the bad, and talk optimistically. By doing so we win over discouragement (Phil. 4:4).

III. Don't Get Down from It

"But thou, O Lord, art . . . the lifter up of mine head" (Ps. 3:3).

A. When Christians neglect to pray and believe God's Word, they are easy prey to discouragement.

B. We must have faith in God. We must ask Him to lift us up and believe that He is able to keep us from falling (Jude 24).

IV. Don't Give Up Through It

"He that endureth to the end shall be saved" (Matt. 10:22).

A. Self-centeredness makes people easy prey to Satan. A lack of love for God and others causes them to give up when discouragement strikes.

B. We must be filled with God's love. Then we must reach out to help the needy and witness to the lost. We can win over discouragement if we "keep on keeping on."

26

You Can Have God's Best

"For God so loved the world, that he gave his only begotten Son, that whosoever believeth in him should not perish, but have everlasting life" (John 3:16).

I. Wonderful Love

"For God so loved the world" (John 3:16).

A. God's love is wonderful because of its outreach. It extends into every nation, city, and town. It reaches into every home, church, and school.

B. God's love is wonderful because of what it does. It delivers from sin, heals the broken hearts, mends hurts and disappointments. It lifts the fallen, restores broken homes (I John 3:1).

II. Wonderful Gift

"that he gave his only begotten Son" (John 3:16).

A. This gift is wonderful because of who He is. Jesus Christ is God's only begotten Son.

B. It is wonderful because of what He did. Jesus gave Himself to die, which was the penalty for man's sins. Not kings, not presidents, not even angels could atone for mankind. Only the blood of Jesus Christ was efficacious.

C. It is wonderful because of what He does. He forgives sins; He cleanses; He gives peace; He loves all mankind—everywhere (I John 4:9).

III. Wonderful Faith

"that whosoever believeth in him should not perish" (John 3:16).

A. Faith is wonderful, for it is the means by which we receive God's wonderful gift, Jesus Christ.

B. Faith pleases God and makes everything possible. We are to live by faith; it is a way of life (I John 5:13).

IV. Wonderful Life

"but have everlasting life" (John 3:16).

A. Life is wonderful because it is God-given. Only God can produce and perfect life.

B. Wonderful life begins when we accept, by faith, God's wonderful love and His wonderful gift.

C. Wonderful life is everlasting. Not even death can separate us from the love of God through Jesus Christ our Lord (Rom. 8:35-39).

27

You Can Win over Temptation

"Blessed is the man that endureth temptation: for when he is tried, he shall receive the crown of life . . ." (James 1:12).

I. With Decision

" . . . every man is tempted, when he is drawn away of his own lust, and enticed" (James 1:14).

A. First, you must decide which way you are going to take—the right or the wrong way. Indecision never wins.

B. Firmness and determination are always necessary if temptation is to be resisted successfully (I Thess. 5:21).

II. With Devotion

" . . . [God] will not suffer you to be tempted above that ye are able . . ." (I Cor. 10:13).

A. The prayers of the righteous prevail. Ask God to help you overcome temptation. Believe that He is doing it—*now*.

B. The promises of God never fail. Jesus overcame temptation by using them. You can overcome by doing likewise (Ps. 119:11).

III. With Discipline

"Blessed is the man that endureth temptation" (James 1:12).

A. Sinful pleasures, pursuits, and practices must be avoided. Stay away from Satan's territory.

B. Set rules and limits for yourself. Practice self-control and restraint. With discipline you can win over much temptation. (I Thess. 5:22).

IV. With Denouncement

"Then saith Jesus unto him, Get thee hence, Satan..."
(Matt. 4:10).

A. When Jesus was tempted, He denounced Satan, saying, "Get thee behind me, Satan" (Luke 4:8).

B. When tempted, we need to do as Jesus did. "Resist the devil, and he will flee from you" (James 4:7).

V. With Diligence

"... lust ... bringeth forth sin: and sin ... bringeth forth death. Do not err, my beloved brethren" (James 1:15, 16).

A. You win over temptation by paying careful attention, by becoming aware of Satan's strategies.

B. You win over temptation through action for God. Become engaged in helping the needy and witnessing to the lost (I Peter 5:8).